GREAT ENGLISH POETS

GREAT ENGLISH POETS

Christina
Rossetti

Edited and with an introduction
by Peter Porter

Clarkson N. Potter, Inc./Publishers NEW YORK
DISTRIBUTED BY CROWN PUBLISHERS, INC.

Selection and Introduction copyright © 1986 by Peter Porter

Published in the United States by Clarkson N. Potter, Inc.,
225 Park Avenue South, New York, New York 10003
and represented in Canada by the Canadian MANDA group
Designed and produced in Great Britain by Aurum Press Ltd.,
33 Museum Street, London WC1A 1LD, England

CLARKSON N. POTTER, POTTER, THE GREAT POETS,
and colophon are trademarks of Clarkson N. Potter, Inc.

Picture research by Juliet Brightmore

Manufactured in Belgium

Library of Congress Cataloging-in-Publication Data
Rossetti, Christina Georgina, 1830–1894.
    Great English poets.
    I. Title.
PR5237.A4   1986   821'.8   86-5037
ISBN 0-517-56288-X

10 9 8 7 6 5 4 3 2 1

First Edition

CONTENTS

INTRODUCTION

Before 1900 the list of women authors in English is short, and of poets, much shorter. Aphra Behn wrote plays and Jane Austen and George Eliot were pre-eminent as novelists. Apart from little known eighteenth-century names, such as those of Mary Leapor and Anna Seward, the feminine authorial roll-call amounts to just Elizabeth Barrett Browning, the Brontë sisters and Christina Rossetti. All were Victorians and, in their several ways, eminently Victorian. The greatest, undoubtedly, was Christina Rossetti, which makes her the finest woman poet in English literature. (Not, of course, in English-language literature. America has Emily Dickinson, and she is one of the supreme poets of all ages and languages.)

It does Christina Rossetti little justice to categorize her as a 'woman poet'. She is a very original writer, resembling almost nobody in her own time. She does not compete with the male poets of the day, even with her brother, Dante Gabriel Rossetti. Influences on her were confined to the Bible and to English and Italian folklore. Yet her sensibility has a directness, a warmth and a passion for truth, which is essentially feminine. She is not a poet of width of experience or great range of interests, but she goes deep.

The Rossettis were a literary family. Christina and her sister and two brothers were three-quarters Italian in origin, and were brought up in a household still wrapped in Italian culture. Her father, Gabriele Rossetti, had been appointed Professor of Italian at King's College, London, after fleeing oppression in his native land at the hand of the Bourbons of Naples. Like many

Italian exiles in England – Foscolo and Alfieri, for instance – Rossetti was a fierce champion of liberty and an opponent of Catholic clericalism. Yet Christina's elder sister became a nun: an Anglican nun, since the children were brought up in the Church of England. The piety which possessed the girls eluded their brothers. Dante Gabriel's feeling for religion was all gilding and romantic attitudinizing. Her other brother, William, who was to be her editor and biographer, was more practical, though he too partook of the revolutionary artistic ethos of the Pre-Raphaelite brotherhood. The Italian half of Christina's mother's parentage resided in the family name, Polidori, which occurs also in the lives of Byron and Shelley.

Despite this Italianness, underlined by the endless comings and goings of Italian exiles at the Rossetti house, Christina's training, at her mother's hands, was in English literature and English piety. Nor is there anything Continental about the aims and aesthetic views of the Pre-Raphaelite brotherhood, other than its name. Languid, sensual, enervating, even consciously decadent on occasions, the Pre-Raphaelites were the most English of all artists. In their rejection of the prevailing tone of Victorianism, they became yet more representatively Victorian. Christina Rossetti was far removed in temperament from the romantic agonies of her brother, of Lizzie Siddell, William and Janey Morris and the Burne-Joneses, but she was as much a lover of detail and of intensity of atmosphere as any of them. Next to Tennyson, she had the best ear of her age. Every one of her poems falls on the reader's senses in an exquisite arrangement of sound. She is repetitive in subject matter – time, death, the seasons, lost love – but her poems work beautiful variations on this traditional material. Above all, she is the poet of daydreaming and longing for the peace and perfection of Paradise. She is a religious poet, but avoids all doctrine and threats.

Christina Rossetti's most famous single poem (an extract from which is included in this selection) is 'Goblin Market'. It is also the poem which made her reputation in her own time, getting her into print before the rest of the Pre-Raphaelites, in 1862. In many ways it is not representative, having a somewhat squashy, overwrought side to it. But it is definitely not a child's poem, being more of an allegory of sensuality, and quite as closely detailed as a painting by Millais or Holman Hunt. Christina's better style is purged of merely 'poetical' language: it is spare, beautifully composed and however dreamy, never inexact. She is also a brilliant handler of stanzas and rhymes.

She was born in London in 1830 and died there in 1894. Twice she might have married, but religious scruples and a retiring personality prevented her. She wrote about the visible changes of season in the English countryside, but she was essentially a city dweller. The prevailing sadness of her verse must reflect the disappointments of her life. But today, a century after her prime, her poetry stands up clearly with all the authority of its truthfulness and its technique. The quiet woman has merged into the established poet.

My Friend

Two days ago with dancing glancing hair,
   With living lips and eyes;
   Now pale, dumb, blind, she lies;
So pale, yet still so fair.

We have not left her yet, not yet alone;
   But soon must leave her where
   She will not miss our care,
Bone of our bone.

Weep not, O friends, we should not weep:
   Our friend of friends lies full of rest;
   No sorrow rankles in her breast,
Fallen fast asleep.

She sleeps below,
   She wakes and laughs above.
   To-day, as she walked, let us walk in love:
To-morrow follow so.

Seasons

In Springtime when the leaves are young,
Clear dewdrops gleam like jewels, hung
On boughs the fair birds roost among.

When Summer comes with sweet unrest,
Birds weary of their mother's breast,
And look abroad and leave the nest.

In Autumn ere the waters freeze,
The swallows fly across the seas:—
If we could fly away with these!

In Winter when the birds are gone,
The sun himself looks starved and wan,
And starved the snow he shines upon.

My Dream

Hear now a curious dream I dreamed last night,
Each word whereof is weighed and sifted truth.

I stood beside Euphrates while it swelled
Like overflowing Jordan in its youth.
It waxed and coloured sensibly to sight;
Till out of myriad pregnant waves there welled
Young crocodiles, a gaunt blunt-featured crew,
Fresh-hatched perhaps and daubed with birthday dew.
The rest if I should tell, I fear my friend,
My closest friend, would deem the facts untrue;
And therefore it were wisely left untold;
Yet if you will, why, hear it to the end.

Each crocodile was girt with massive gold
And polished stones that with their wearers grew:
But one there was who waxed beyond the rest,
Wore kinglier girdle and a kingly crown,
Whilst crowns and orbs and sceptres starred his
    breast.
All gleamed compact and green with scale on scale,
But special burnishment adorned his mail
And special terror weighed upon his frown;
His punier brethren quaked before his tail,
Broad as a rafter, potent as a flail.
So he grew lord and master of his kin:
But who shall tell the tale of all their woes?
An execrable appetite arose,
He battened on them, crunched, and sucked them in.

He knew no law, he feared no binding law,
But ground them with inexorable jaw.
The luscious fat distilled upon his chin,
Exuded from his nostrils and his eyes,
While still like hungry death he fed his maw;
Till, every minor crocodile being dead
And buried too, himself gorged to the full,
He slept with breath oppressed and unstrung claw.

Oh marvel passing strange which next I saw!
In sleep he dwindled to the common size,
And all the empire faded from his coat.
Then from far off a wingèd vessel came,
Swift as a swallow, subtle as a flame:
I know not what it bore of freight or host,
But white it was as an avenging ghost.
It levelled strong Euphrates in its course;
Supreme yet weightless as an idle mote
It seemed to tame the waters without force
Till not a murmur swelled or billow beat.
Lo, as the purple shadow swept the sands,
The prudent crocodile rose on his feet,
And shed appropriate tears and wrung his hands.
What can it mean? you ask. I answer not
For meaning, but myself must echo, What?
And tell it as I saw it on the spot.

Looking Forward

Sleep, let me sleep, for I am sick of care;
   Sleep, let me sleep, for my pain wearies me.
Shut out the light; thicken the heavy air
With drowsy incense; let a distant stream
Of music lull me, languid as a dream,
   Soft as the whisper of a summer sea.

Pluck me no rose that groweth on a thorn,
   Nor myrtle white and cold as snow in June,
Fit for a virgin on her marriage morn:
But bring me poppies brimmed with sleepy death,
And ivy choking what it garlandeth,
   And primroses that open to the moon.

Listen, the music swells into a song,
   A simple song I loved in days of yore;
The echoes take it up and up along
The hills, and the wind blows it back again. –
Peace, peace, there is a memory in that strain
   Of happy days that shall return no more.

Oh peace! your music wakeneth old thought,
   But not old hope that made my life so sweet,
Only the longing that must end in nought.
Have patience with me, friends, a little while:
For soon, where you shall dance and sing and smile,
   My quickened dust may blossom at your feet.

Sweet thought that I may yet live and grow green,
  That leaves may yet spring from the withered root,
And buds and flowers and berries half unseen.
Then, if you haply muse upon the past,
Say this: Poor child, she has her wish at last;
  Barren through life, but in death bearing fruit.

A Pause

They made the chamber sweet with flowers
    and leaves,
  And the bed sweet with flowers on which I lay;
  While my soul, love-bound, loitered on its way.
I did not hear the birds about the eaves,
Nor hear the reapers talk among the sheaves:
  Only my soul kept watch from day to day,
  My thirsty soul kept watch for one away:—
Perhaps he loves, I thought, remembers, grieves.
At length there came the step upon the stair,
  Upon the lock the old familiar hand:
Then first my spirit seemed to scent the air
  Of Paradise; then first the tardy sand
Of time ran golden; and I felt my hair
  Put on a glory, and my soul expand.

Amor Mundi

'Oh, where are you going with your lovelocks
    flowing,
  On the west wind blowing along this valley track?'
'The downhill path is easy, come with me an' it
    please ye,
  We shall escape the uphill by never turning back.'

So they two went together in glowing August weather,
  The honey-breathing heather lay to their left and
    right;
And dear she was to dote on, her swift feet seemed to
    float on
  The air like soft twin pigeons too sportive to alight.

'Oh, what is that in heaven where grey cloudflakes are
    seven,
  Where blackest clouds hang riven just at the rainy
    skirt?'
'Oh, that's a meteor sent us, a message dumb,
    portentous,
  An undecipher'd solemn signal of help or hurt.'

'Oh, what is that glides quickly where velvet flowers
    grow thickly,
  Their scent comes rich and sickly?' 'A scaled and
    hooded worm.'
'Oh, what's that in the hollow, so pale I quake to
    follow?'
    'Oh, that's a thin dead body, which awaits the
    eternal term.'

'Turn again, O my sweetest,—turn again, false and
    fleetest:
  This beaten way thou beatest I fear is hell's own
    track.'
'Nay, too steep for hill-mounting; nay, too late for
    cost counting:
  This downhill path is easy, but there's no turning
    back.'

In the Lane

When my love came home to me,
  Pleasant summer bringing,
Every tree was out in leaf,
  Every bird was singing.

There I met her in the lane
  By those waters gleamy,
Met her toward the fall of day,
  Warm and dear and dreamy.
Did I loiter in the lane?
  None was there to see me.

Only roses in the hedge,
  Lilies on the river,
Saw our greeting fast and fond,
  Counted gift and giver,
Saw me take her to my home,
  Take her home forever.

Goblin Market

Morning and evening
Maids heard the goblins cry:
'Come buy our orchard fruits,
Come buy, come buy:
Apples and quinces,
Lemons and oranges,
Plump unpecked cherries,
Melons and raspberries,
Bloom-down-cheeked peaches,
Swart-headed mulberries,
Wild free-born cranberries,
Crab-apples, dewberries,
Pine-apples, blackberries,
Apricots, strawberries;–
All ripe together
In summer weather,–
Morns that pass by,
Fair eves that fly;
Come buy, come buy:
Our grapes fresh from the vine,
Pomegranates full and fine,
Dates and sharp bullaces,
Rare pears and greengages,
Damsons and bilberries,
Taste them and try:
Currants and gooseberries,
Bright-fire-like barberries,
Figs to fill your mouth,

Citrons from the South,
Sweet to tongue and sound to eye;
Come buy, come buy.'

Evening by evening
Among the brookside rushes,
Laura bowed her head to hear,
Lizzie veiled her blushes:
Crouching close together
In the cooling weather,
With clasping arms and cautioning lips,
With tingling cheeks and finger tips.
'Lie close,' Laura said,
Pricking up her golden head:
'We must not look at goblin men,
We must not buy their fruits:
Who knows upon what soil they fed
Their hungry thirsty roots?'
'Come buy,' call the goblins
Hobbling down the glen.
'Oh,' cried Lizzie, 'Laura, Laura,
You should not peep at goblin men.'
Lizzie covered up her eyes,
Covered close lest they should look;
Laura reared her glossy head,
And whispered like the restless brook:
'Look, Lizzie, look, Lizzie,
Down the glen tramp little men.
One hauls a basket,
One bears a plate,

One lugs a golden dish
Of many pounds weight.
How fair the vine must grow
Whose grapes are so luscious;
How warm the wind must blow
Through those fruit bushes.'
'No,' said Lizzie: 'No, no, no;
Their offers should not charm us,
Their evil gifts would harm us.'
She thrust a dimpled finger
In each ear, shut eyes and ran:
Curious Laura chose to linger
Wondering at each merchant man.
One had a cat's face,
One whisked a tail,
One tramped at a rat's pace,
One crawled like a snail,
One like a wombat prowled obtuse and furry,
One like a ratel tumbled hurry skurry.
She heard a voice like voice of doves
Cooing all together:
They sounded kind and full of loves
In the pleasant weather.

Laura stretched her gleaming neck
Like a rush-imbedded swan,
Like a lily from the beck,
Like a moonlit poplar branch,
Like a vessel at the launch
When its last restraint is gone.

A Birthday

My heart is like a singing bird
    Whose nest is in a watered shoot:
My heart is like an apple-tree
    Whose boughs are bent with thickset fruit;
My heart is like a rainbow shell
    That paddles in a halcyon sea;
My heart is gladder than all these
    Because my love is come to me.

Raise me a dais of silk and down;
    Hang it with vair and purple dyes;
Carve it in doves and pomegranates,
    And peacocks with a hundred eyes;
Work it in gold and silver grapes,
    In leaves and silver fleurs-de-lys;
Because the birthday of my life
    Is come, my love is come to me.

Luscious and Sorrowful

Beautiful, tender, wasting away for sorrow;
Thus today; and how shall it be with thee tomorrow?
    Beautiful, tender—what else?
        A hope tells.

Beautiful, tender, keeping the jubilee
In the land of home together, past death and sea;
    No more change or death, no more
        Salt sea-shore.

Eve

'While I sit at the door,
Sick to gaze within,
Mine eye weepeth sore
For sorrow and sin:
As a tree my sin stands
To darken all lands;
Death is the fruit it bore.

'How have Eden bowers grown
Without Adam to bend them?
How have Eden flowers blown,
Squandering their sweet breath,
Without me to tend them?
The Tree of Life was ours,
Tree twelvefold-fruited,
Most lofty tree that flowers,
Most deeply rooted:
I chose the Tree of Death.

'Hadst thou but said me nay,
    Adam my brother,
I might have pined away—
    I, but none other:
God might have let thee stay
Safe in our garden,
By putting me away
Beyond all pardon.

'I, Eve, sad mother
Of all who must live,

I, not another,
Plucked bitterest fruit to give
My friend, husband, lover.
O wanton eyes, run over!
Who but I should grieve?
Cain hath slain his brother:
Of all who must die mother,
Miserable Eve!'

Thus she sat weeping,
Thus Eve our mother,
Where one lay sleeping
Slain by his brother.
Greatest and least
Each piteous beast
To hear her voice
Forgot his joys
And set aside his feast.

The mouse paused in his walk
And dropped his wheaten stalk;
Grave cattle wagged their heads
In rumination;
The eagle gave a cry
From his cloud station:
Larks on thyme beds
Forbore to mount or sing;
Bees drooped upon the wing;
The raven perched on high
Forgot his ration;
The conies in their rock,

A feeble nation,
Quaked sympathetical;
The mocking-bird left off to mock;
Huge camels knelt as if
In deprecation;
The kind hart's tears were falling;
Chattered the wistful stork;
Dove-voices with a dying fall
Cooed desolation,
Answering grief by grief.

Only the serpent in the dust,
Wriggling and crawling,
Grinned an evil grin and thrust
His tongue out with its fork.

Lines from
'What Good Shall My Life Do Me?'

Love in the gracious rain distils:
Love moves the subtle fountain-rills
To fertilize uplifted hills,

And seedful valleys fertilize:
Love stills the hungry lion's cries,
And the young raven satisfies:

Love hangs this earth in space: Love rolls
Fair worlds rejoicing on their poles,
And girds them round with aureoles:

Love lights the sun: Love through the dark
Lights the moon's evanescent arc:
Same Love lights up the glow-worm's spark:

Love rears the great: Love tends the small:
Breaks off the yoke, breaks down the wall:
Accepteth all, fulfilleth all.

O ye who taste that Love is sweet,
Set waymarks for the doubtful feet
That stumble on in search of it.

Sing hymns of Love, that those who hear
Far off in pain may lend an ear,
Rise up and wonder and draw near.

Lead lives of Love, that others who
Behold your lives may kindle too
With Love and cast their lots with you.

Up-hill

Does the road wind up-hill all the way?
  Yes, to the very end.
Will the day's journey take the whole long day?
  From morn to night, my friend.

But is there for the night a resting-place?
  A roof for when the slow dark hours begin.
May not the darkness hide it from my face?
  You cannot miss that inn.

Shall I meet other wayfarers at night?
  Those who have gone before.
Then must I knock, or call when just in sight?
  They will not keep you standing at that door.

Shall I find comfort, travel-sore and weak?
  Of labour you shall find the sum.
Will there be beds for me and all who seek?
  Yea, beds for all who come.

The Queen of Hearts

How comes it, Flora, that, whenever we
Play cards together, you invariably,
    However the pack parts,
    Still hold the Queen of Hearts?

I've scanned you with a scrutinizing gaze,
Resolved to father these your secret ways:
    But sift them as I will,
    Your ways are secret still.

I cut and shuffle; shuffle, cut, again;
But all my cutting, shuffling, proves in vain:
    Vain hope, vain forethought too;
    That Queen still falls to you.

I dropped her once, prepense; but, ere the deal
Was dealt, your instinct seemed her loss to feel:
    'There should be one card more,'
    You said, and searched the floor.

I cheated once; I made a private notch
In Heart-Queen's back, and kept a lynx-eyed watch;
    Yet such another back
    Deceived me in the pack:

The Queen of Clubs assumed by arts unknown
An imitative dint that seemed my own;
    This notch, not of my doing,
    Misled me to my ruin.

It baffles me to puzzle out the clue,
  Which must be skill, or craft, or luck in you:
    Unless, indeed, it be
    Natural affinity.

Stanzas from 'Three Stages'

The fruitless thought of what I might have been,
  Haunting me ever, will not let me rest.
A cold North wind has withered all my green,
  My sun is in the West.

But, where my palace stood, with the same stone
  I will uprear a shady hermitage:
And there my spirit shall keep house alone,
  Accomplishing its age.

There other garden-beds shall lie around,
  Full of sweet-briar and incense-bearing thyme:
There will I sit, and listen for the sound
  Of the last lingering chime.

Echo

Come to me in the silence of the night;
　Come in the speaking silence of a dream:
Come with soft rounded cheeks and eyes as bright
　As sunlight on a stream;
　　Come back in tears,
O memory, hope, love of finished years.

Oh dream how sweet, too sweet, too bitter sweet,
　Whose wakening should have been in Paradise,
Where souls brimfull of love abide and meet;
　Where thirsting longing eyes
　　Watch the slow door
That opening, letting in, lets out no more.

Yet come to me in dreams, that I may live
　My very life again though cold in death:
Come back to me in dreams, that I may give
　Pulse for pulse, breath for breath:
　　Speak low, lean low,
As long ago, my love, how long ago!

The Heart Knoweth Its Own Bitterness

When all the over-work of life
  Is finished once, and fast·asleep
We swerve no more beneath the knife
  But taste that silence cool and deep;
Forgetful of the highways rough,
  Forgetful of the thorny scourge,
  Forgetful of the tossing surge,
Then shall we find it is enough?

How can we say 'enough' on earth—
  'Enough' with such a craving heart?
I have not found it since my birth,
  But still have bartered part for part.
I have not held and hugged the whole,
  But paid the old to gain the new:
  Much have I paid, yet much is due,
Till I am beggared sense and soul.

I used to labour, used to strive
  For pleasure with a restless will:
Now if I save my soul alive
  All else what matters, good or ill?
I used to dream alone, to plan
  Unspoken hopes and days to come:—
  Of all my past this is the sum—
I will not lean on child of man.

To give, to give, not to receive!
  I long to pour myself, my soul,
Not to keep back or count or leave,

But king with king to give the whole.
I long for one to stir my deep—
    I have had enough of help and gift—
    I long for one to search and sift
Myself, to take myself and keep.

You scratch my surface with your pin,
    You stroke me smooth with hushing breath:—
Nay pierce, nay probe, nay dig within,
    Probe my quick core and sound my depth.
You call me with a puny call,
    You talk, you smile, you nothing do:
    How should I spend my heart on you,
My heart that so outweighs you all?

Your vessels are by much too strait:
    Were I to pour, you could not hold.—
Bear with me: I must bear to wait,
    A fountain sealed through heat and cold.
Bear with me days or months or years:
    Deep must call deep until the end
    When friend shall no more envy friend
Nor vex his friend at unawares.

Not in this world of hope deferred,
    This world of perishable stuff:—
Eye hath not seen nor ear hath heard
    Nor heart conceived that full 'enough':
Here moans the separating sea,
    Here harvests fail, here breaks the heart:
    There God shall join and no man part,
I full of Christ and Christ of me.

Pastime

A boat amid the ripples, drifting, rocking;
Two idle people, without pause or aim;
While in the ominous West there gathers darkness
    Flushed with flame.

A hay-cock in a hay-field, backing, lapping;
Two drowsy people pillowed round-about;
While in the ominous West across the darkness
    Flame leaps out.

Better a wrecked life than a life so aimless,
Better a wrecked life than a life so soft:
The ominous West glooms thundering, with its fire
    Lit aloft.

Somewhere or Other

Somewhere or other there must surely be
    The face not seen, the voice not heard,
The heart that not yet–never yet–ah me!
    Made answer to my word.

Somewhere or other, may be near or far;
    Past land and sea, clean out of sight;
Beyond the wandering moon, beyond the star
    That tracks her night by night.

Somewhere or other, may be far or near;
    With just a wall, a hedge, between;
With just the last leaves of the dying year
    Fallen on a turf grown green.

Memory

1

I nursed it in my bosom while it lived,
  I hid it in my heart when it was dead.
In joy I sat alone; even so I grieved
    Alone, and nothing said.

I shut the door to face the naked truth,
  I stood alone—I faced the truth alone,
Stripped bare of self-regard or forms or ruth
    Till first and last were shown.

I took the perfect balances and weighed;
  No shaking of my hand disturbed the poise;
Weighed, found it wanting: not a word I said,
    But silent made my choice.

None know the choice I made; I make it still.
  None know the choice I made and broke my heart,
Breaking mine idol: I have braced my will
    Once, chosen for once my part.

I broke it at a blow, I laid it cold,
  Crushed in my deep heart where it used to live.
My heart dies inch by inch; the time grows old,
    Grows old in which I grieve.

2

I have a room whereinto no one enters
  Save I myself alone:
  There sits a blessed memory on a throne,
There my life centres;

While winter comes and goes—oh tedious comer!—
  And while its nip-wind blows;
  While bloom the bloodless lily and warm rose
Of lavish summer.

If any should force entrance he might see there
  One buried yet not dead,
  Before whose face I no more bow my head
Or bend my knee there;

But often in my worn life's autumn weather
  I watch there with clear eyes,
  And think how it will be in Paradise
When we're together.

L.E.L.
'Whose heart was breaking for a little love.'

Downstairs I laugh, I sport and jest with all;
  But in my solitary room above
I turn my face in silence to the wall;
  My heart is breaking for a little love.
    Though winter frosts are done,
    And birds pair every one,
And leaves peep out, for springtide is begun.

I feel no spring, while spring is well-nigh blown,
  I find no nest, while nests are in the grove:
Woe's me for mine own heart that dwells alone,
  My heart that breaketh for a little love.
    While golden in the sun
    Rivulets rise and run,
While lilies bud, for springtide is begun.

All love, are loved, save only I; their hearts
  Beat warm with love and joy, beat full thereof:
They cannot guess, who play the pleasant parts,
  My heart is breaking for a little love.
    While bee-hives wake and whirr,
    And rabbit thins his fur,
In living spring that sets the world astir.

I deck myself with silks and jewelry,
  I plume myself like any mated dove:
They praise my rustling show, and never see
  My heart is breaking for a little love.

While sprouts green lavender
With rosemary and myrrh,
For in quick spring the sap is all astir.

Perhaps some saints in glory guess the truth,
Perhaps some angels read it as they move,
And cry one to another full of ruth,
'Her heart is breaking for a little love.'
Though other things have birth,
And leap and sing for mirth,
When springtime wakes and clothes and feeds the
earth.

Yet saith a saint, 'Take patience for thy scythe';
Yet saith an angel: 'Wait, and thou shalt prove
True best is last, true life is born of death,
O thou, heart-broken for a little love.
Then love shall fill thy girth,
And love make fat thy dearth,
When new spring builds new heaven and clean new
earth.'

A Triad

Three sang of love together: one with lips
 Crimson, with cheeks and bosom in a glow,
Flushed to the yellow hair and finger-tips;
 And one there sang who soft and smooth as snow
 Bloomed like a tinted hyacinth at a show;
And one was blue with famine after love,
 Who like a harpstring snapped rang harsh and low
The burden of what those were singing of.
One shamed herself in love; one temperately
 Grew gross in soulless love, a sluggish wife;
One famished died for love. Thus two of three
 Took death for love and won him after strife;
One droned in sweetness like a fattened bee:
 All on the threshold, yet all short of life.

A Christmas Carol

In the bleak mid-winter
  Frosty wind made moan,
Earth stood hard as iron,
  Water like a stone;
Snow had fallen, snow on snow,
  Snow on snow,
In the bleak mid-winter
  Long ago.

Our God, Heaven cannot hold Him
  Nor earth sustain;
Heaven and earth shall flee away
  When he comes to reign:
In the bleak mid-winter
  A stable-place sufficed
The Lord God Almighty
  Jesus Christ.

Enough for Him, whom cherubim
  Worship night and day,
A breastful of milk
  And a mangerful of hay;
Enough for Him, whom angels
  Fall down before,
The ox and ass and camel
  Which adore.

Angels and archangels
  May have gathered there,
Cherubim and seraphim
  Thronged the air;
But only His mother
  In her maiden bliss
Worshipped the Beloved
  With a kiss.

What can I give Him,
  Poor as I am?
If I were a shepherd
  I would bring a lamb,
If I were a Wise Man
  I would do my part,—
Yet what I can I give Him,
  Give my heart.

Mary Magdalene

She came in deep repentance,
    And knelt down at His feet
Who can change the sorrow into joy,
    The bitter into sweet.

She had cast away her jewels
    And her rich attire,
And her breast was filled with a holy shame,
    And her heart with a holy fire.

Her tears were more precious
    Than her precious pearls—
Her tears that fell upon His feet
    As she wiped them with her curls.

Her youth and her beauty
    Were budding to their prime;
But she wept for the great transgression,
    The sin of other time.

Trembling betwixt hope and fear,
    She sought the King of Heaven,
Forsook the evil of her ways,
    Loved much, and was forgiven.

Twilight Calm

Oh pleasant eventide!
Clouds on the western side
Grow grey and greyer, hiding the warm sun:
The bees and birds, their happy labours done,
    Seek their close nests and bide.

Screened in the leafy wood
The stock-doves sit and brood:
The very squirrel leaps from bough to bough
But lazily; pauses; and settles now
    Where once he stored his food.

One by one the flowers close,
Lily and dewy rose
Shutting their tender petals from the moon:
The grasshoppers are still; but not so soon
    Are still the noisy crows.

The dormouse squats and eats
Choice little dainty bits
Beneath the spreading roots of a broad lime;
Nibbling his fill he stops from time to time
    And listens where he sits.

From far the lowings come
Of cattle driven home:
From farther still the wind brings fitfully
The vast continual murmur of the sea,
    Now loud, now almost dumb.

The gnats whirl in the air,
The evening gnats; and there
The owl opes broad his eyes and wings to sail
For prey; the bat wakes; and the shell-less snail
Comes forth, clammy and bare.

Hark! that's the nightingale,
Telling the self-same tale
Her song told when this ancient earth was young:
So echoes answered when her song was sung
In the first wooded vale.

We call it love and pain,
The passion of her strain;
And yet we little understand or know:
Why should it not be rather joy that so
Throbs in each throbbing vein?

In separate herds the deer
Lie; here the bucks, and here
The does, and by its mother sleeps the fawn:
Through all the hours of night until the dawn
They sleep, forgetting fear.

The hare sleeps where it lies,
With wary half-closed eyes;
The cock has ceased to crow, the hen to cluck:
Only the fox is out, some heedless duck
Or chicken to surprise.

Remote, each single star
Comes out, till there they are
All shining brightly. How the dews fall damp!
While close at hand the glow-worm lights her lamp,
Or twinkles from afar.

But evening now is done
As much as if the sun
Day-giving had arisen in the East—
For night has come; and the great calm has ceased,
The quiet sands have run.

Song

When I am dead, my dearest,
  Sing no sad songs for me;
Plant thou no roses at my head,
  Nor shady cypress tree:
Be the green grass above me
  With showers and dewdrops wet:
And if thou wilt, remember,
  And if thou wilt, forget.

I shall not see the shadows,
  I shall not fear the rain;
I shall not hear the nightingale
  Sing on as if in pain:
And dreaming through the twilight
  That doth not rise nor set,
Haply I may remember,
  And haply may forget.

NOTES ON THE PICTURES

p.6 Walter Crane (1845–1915). *Madonna Lilies in a Garden*, 1908. Oil on canvas.
Private Collection. Photo: Bridgeman Art Library, London.

p.15 Frederick Walker (1840–75). *Spring*, 1864. Watercolour.
Reproduced by courtesy of the Board of Trustees of the Victoria and Albert Museum, London.

p.18 Dante Gabriel Rossetti (1828–82). *Beata Beatrix*, 1864–70. Oil on canvas.
Reproduced by permission of the Trustees of the Tate Gallery, London.

p.23 Frederick Smallfield (1829–1915). *Early Lovers*, 1858. Oil on canvas.
Reproduced by permission of City of Manchester Art Galleries.

p.26 Arthur Rackham (1867–1939). *White and Golden Lizzie Stood*. Book illustration from an edition of *Goblin Market*, 1933.
© Harrap Ltd, London.

p.31 J. R. Spencer Stanhope (1829–1908). *Eve Tempted*, exhibited 1877. Tempera on panel.
Reproduced by permission of City of Manchester Art Galleries.

p.35 Edward Burne-Jones (1833–98). *Ladder of Heaven*, 1882–98. Watercolour.
Reproduced by permission of the Trustees of the British Museum, London.

p.38 Francis Danby (1793–1861). *Disappointed Love*, exhibited 1821. Oil on panel.
Reproduced by courtesy of the Board of Trustees of the Victoria and Albert Museum, London.

p.43 Dante Gabriel Rossetti. *Reverie*, 1868. Coloured chalks.
Reproduced by courtesy of Christie's, London. Photo: Bridgeman Art Library, London.

p.46 Richard Redgrave (1804–88). *The Governess*, 1844. Oil on canvas.
Reproduced by courtesy of the Board of Trustees of the Victoria and Albert Museum, London.

p.51 Alexander Mann (1853–1908). *The New Baby*, c. 1886–8. Oil on canvas.
Reproduced by courtesy of The Fine Art Society, London.

p.55 William J. Webbe (*fl.* 1853–78). *Twilight*, date unknown. Oil on canvas.
Private collection. Photo: Bridgeman Art Library, London.

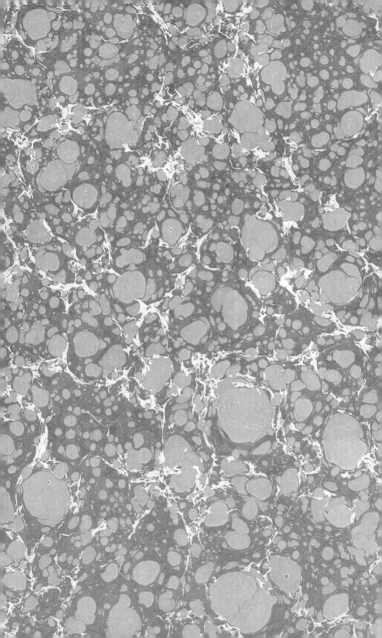